harrison ford

© Fitway Publishing, 2007
Original editions in English, French and Spanish

Translations: Translate-A-Book, Oxford
Maria Sol Kliczkowski, Madrid

Design: GRAPH'M/Nord Compo, France
Garnas Design, USA

Production: Patty Holden Productions

ISBN: 978-2-7528-0247-7

Printed in Korea

www.silverbackbooks.com

Fitway Publishing, imprint of Silverback Books, Inc.
55 New Montgomery Street, Suite 500
San Francisco, CA 94105 USA

TO ANOUK

harrison
ford

laurence caracalla

contents

"I conduct my profession the way I make furniture. There's no tricks, no magic, no mysteries. There's nothing but work, willpower, technique, and lots and lots of patience."

Everything has been said about him and, at the same time, nothing. He's a star, a legend even. He's also an ordinary man and occasional carpenter. But who is the real Harrison Ford? He's a private person. Filmmaking is his job, that's all. Don't ask more of him than that. The Hollywood nights and the gala premiers mean very little to him. Above all, he's an actor. "I conduct my profession the way I make furniture. There's no tricks, no magic, no mysteries. There's nothing but work, willpower, technique, and lots and lots of patience." He understands patience. He didn't become famous until he was thirty-five, the age when others are already on their way down. Han Solo, his character in *Star Wars*, made him a superstar. He masterfully conducted his career by following up with another cult role as *Indiana Jones*. Now over 60, he is once again ready to wear the uniform of Hollywood's most celebrated adventurer. It's easy to imagine what the actor will make of his aging character. He'll be the same as before, sexy, funny, foolhardy without really meaning to be, sometimes even a little tormented.

Harrison Ford will never lose sight of his priorities: to pursue his career with passion and seriousness. It's a trademark of his, along with the famous scar, that marks his chin.

Harrison Ford, legendary hero....
and carpenter

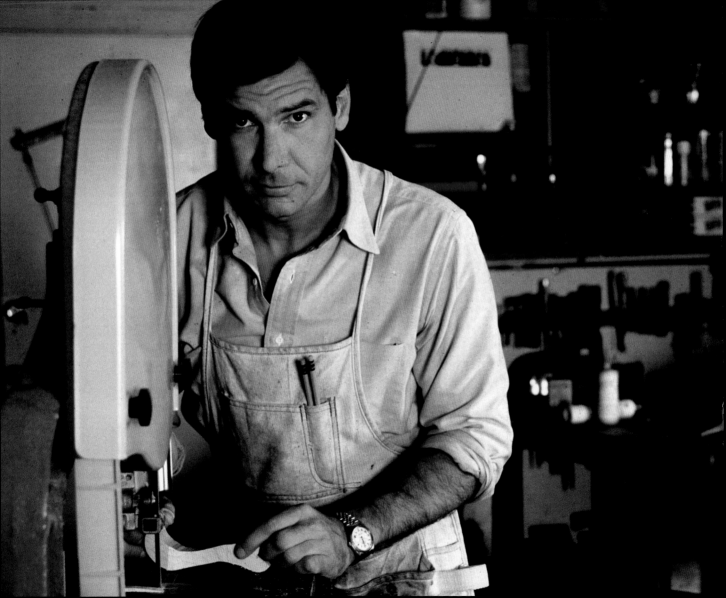

Getting Straight, *1970.*

n the Ford family, don't expect to find Glenn, one of the most popular actors of the 1950s, or John, the legendary director of westerns, or even Henry, inventor of the automobile. They're no relation. The Chicago Fords are a family like any other, or almost. Harrison's father, Christopher, was Irish-Catholic and a TV advertising executive. His mother, Dorothy, is a Russian Jew who gave birth to Harrison on July 13, 1942, naming him after his maternal great-grandfather. A second child, Terence, was born four years later.

Although Harrison has one grandfather who was a vaudeville and radio comedian and acted in cabarets, the Ford family is basically middle-class. Harrison felt no inclination to follow in the footsteps of his performing forebear. He didn't feel like doing much of anything. He was a mediocre student, and rather shy according to highschool friends. If he went to the movies, it was more to see the popular actresses of the day than out of any kind of taste for cinema, strictly speaking. Acting was the last thing on his mind. At the insistence of his parents, he enrolled at Ripon College in Wisconsin in 1960 where he studied English literature and philosophy. His grades were disastrous. In his third year, the only way to bring up his average was to enroll in drama class. It was just a class like any other that the inveterate dunce thought would be a cinch. He forgot that it meant getting up on the stage, a fact that didn't exactly thrill him, and even terrified him. He tried to remain inconspicuous in hopes of being ignored. He was even negligent about his courses, which he thought were "of no use." But, as he moved from one small role to the next, he started to imagine a career. When he appeared in Tennessee Williams's *Night of the Iguana*, it wasn't a huge turning point, but it was the birth of a desire. Why not stride the boards? Just don't tell him he was following in the footsteps of his grandfather. No, it was chance and only chance that led him to become an actor. So it was set, he'd found his career. His parents were skeptical but they encouraged him, as did his girlfriend, also a budding actress. He'd met this girl, Mary Marquardt, several years earlier and they had become inseparable. In June 1964, Harrison

*Harrison Ford and wife, Mary
Marquardt, walking in New York City*

abandoned his studies only months before graduation. He was noticed and hired by Bill Fucik,

who directed the Belfry Theatre. At 21, he played all the major roles on the theater program.

He finally had a chance to assert himself, but he knew very well that Wisconsin was not the place

to launch an illustrious career.

Harrison and Mary were wed. The young couple decided their future by tossing a

coin. Tails meant New York, the theater, and playing the same role night after night; heads meant

Hollywood, movies, and television. Tails represented glacial winters, and heads was constant

sunshine. It was a difficult choice and the coin toss went awry. New York won. So they tossed it

again and again until they were finally Hollywood-bound, as "destiny" would have it.

How do you make it in Hollywood if you aren't willing to do just anything that comes along—and no one is waiting on a street corner to offer you the role of a lifetime? You wait, you get bored, and you get a little desperate, but not too much. This wasn't Harrison Ford's style. It was even less his style to run from audition to audition, waiting for his ship to come in. Then, on one of those depressing days when Harrison had lost all faith, a producer at Columbia gave him a seven-year contract for $150 a week as part of their New Talent Program. To earn his pay, he had to do everything he disliked, such as posing with gorgeous women, escorting them to premiers, and imitating the stars of the time. It was horrible! He didn't resemble anyone, he didn't want to resemble anyone. He was found to be temperamental and even "strange," a dangerous adjective in Hollywood. His career took a disastrous turn. He himself admits that he wasn't very cooperative. One day they gave him an Elvis hairstyle and the next, asked him to change his name. It was hell. He was just one step away from abandoning his career. Nevertheless, he accepted roles on *Ironside* and *The Virginian*. He was unhappy and made those around him miserable, too. In 1966, he was hired to play a bellhop in *Dead Heat on a Merry-Go-Round*. A studio big shot called him into his office–could this be the start of a real career? What he told Harrison was, "When Tony Curtis first walked onscreen carrying a bag of groceries—a bag of groceries!—you took one look at him and said, that's a movie star!" What Harrison said in response was, "Weren't you supposed to say, that's a grocery delivery boy?" He was fired on the spot. "Maybe you're not made for this profession." He was sure that he was.

Finally, he received the only good news of 1966, that he would not be going to Vietnam. He was a conscientious objector and did not want to participate in a war he didn't understand. So he wrote a long, pseudo-philosophical letter to the authorities explaining his reasons. "I confused them so badly that they never took action on my petition." At home, while waiting to build a career, he started building furniture.

At first glance, it appears that Jacques Demy, the director of *Parapluies de Cherbourg* (*The Umbrellas of Cherbourg*), and Harrison Ford inhabit two very different universes. And yet in 1968, the French filmmaker was summoned to Hollywood. The American producers asked him to make a sequel to Lola, his most famous film, with Anouk Aimé. She would be part of the production in any case, but they needed an actor to play the young American with whom she would fall in love. Jacques Demy began casting and settled on a newcomer who was handsome, funny and talented, and who quickly became a close friend of the Frenchman and his wife, Agnès Varda. Thus he chose Harrison Ford to be the star of *Model Shop*. He even took his new hire to research the film. The two friends visited those strange establishments where amateur photographers could photograph nude girls. Harrison would later describe their embarrassment when they were visited at their places of business by the "professionals." At the last minute, a producer declared that poor Harrison Ford had no future in cinema and refused to hire him. He forced Jacques Demy to use another actor, Gary Lockwood, who had just finished making *2001, A Space Odyssey* with Kubrick. Jacques Demy would always be mortified by this decision that was made over his head. The film was a flop. As for the producer who saw absolutely no charisma in the young actor, he certainly had a nose for talent! Many years later, Agnès Varda and the star had a good laugh, speculating what would have happened to *Model Shop* if Ford had been chosen for the role.

The Fords weren't exactly rolling in money, even after Harrison signed a new contract, this time with Universal. He had to feed his growing family (Mary gave birth to their first son, Benjamin, in 1967, and then to Willard in 1969). Ford was a responsible guy. He needed a job, even if it wasn't in movies. While fixing up his dilapidated house, Harrison had the somewhat hasty idea of becoming a carpenter. There weren't very many in Hollywood and the people there always had plenty of money and things that needed fixing. To get himself started, he read all the books on the subject. He then had the chutzpah to offer to build a recording studio for the Brazilian musician Sergio Mendes. "I had the right costume, I had the right attitudes, he forgot to ask me, if I'd ever done it before." He turned out to be a natural.

Harrison Ford was the one to hire in Hollywood, a good address for actors, producers, and directors. It wasn't exactly the kind of fame he was looking for, but it was fame nonetheless. He continued this activity for eight years, during which he had very few parts, among them a role with Antonioni that would land on the cutting room floor, and the hit movie *American Graffiti*. He says those years of sanding wood taught him a lot about aesthetics, discipline, and appreciation of a job well done. This appreciation would serve him well in his future career. Dressed as a carpenter, he was finally himself. Building and restoring, he was redeemed in his own eyes. After piling failure on top of failure, Harrison was starting to feel frustrated, or "insufferable" as his friends would say. He finally came into his own. Was it just that he'd proved he was good for something?

Returning from a job, Harrison Ford lost control of his truck and ran into a telephone pole. The doctor who treated him repaired his bloody chin as best he could. "That guy was a butcher," Ford would later say. Harrison was certain that these stitches would spell the end of any career prospects for a young actor in Hollywood. He would become much more than that, and maybe it was even because of these scars, which he never attempted to cover up. They were his stigmata, as famous as Kirk Douglas' dimple, a mark of sex appeal, and certainly not an obstacle to his career, as he then feared.

Of course, he didn't play a major role, but it was a start. *American Graffiti* was an international success and would change Harrison Ford's life. More than anything else, he owed it to his career in carpentry. Fred Roos was the casting director for Francis Ford Coppola. In exchange for working on his house, he kept the actor informed of any interesting auditions. He

American Graffiti *(1973),*
the first real part

was the one who suggested Ford try auditioning for Coppola, producer of the George Lucas film. This was in 1972, when Harrison was thirty-years old, and starting to lose patience. He wasn't very enthusiastic about the audition. He was hired to play Bob Falfa, a sort of young hooligan hidden under a cowboy hat (he was also the one who suggested the hat to Lucas). The role was small and badly paid. He was the oldest actor in the film, as well as the most highly motivated. His fellow actors remember drunken nights and even drunken drives organized by Harrison. For him, the stakes were low because he never for a moment anticipated the success that *American Graffiti* would have, or that he would be noticed. The film's producers took in 120 million dollars at the box office. Harrison pocketed 400 dollars for two weeks of filming, nothing to write home about. When filming was over, the furniture maker returned to his craft.

However, he had now met George Lucas, who remembered him not only as a talented actor, but for his astute observations on the set. In Ford, he sensed a committed actor. Nothing came of it at the time, but Lucas didn't forget him.

Even if the public didn't remember his name, Harrison was more determined than ever. A few months later, he was hired for the next Coppola film, *The Conversation*, with Gene Hackman. He was initially chosen for an important role that was eventually played by Frederic Forrest. The director, slightly embarrassed, decided to keep him on the set and wrote him a very small part. Harrison was furious. He felt that he'd been had. So he decided to flesh out this character by inventing an entire back story. He would be homosexual, crazy, and jealous of his boss, Robert Duvall. Coppola, at first taken aback, accepted all the actor's suggestions. Although, the role was still small, it was now more interesting than it had been. For the first time, the name of Harrison Ford was making the rounds in Hollywood as an actor, rather than as a carpenter.

George Lucas was preparing the biggest film of his life. He'd been thinking about it for years. It would be a "space western." Coppola was producing and casting began. Once

again, Fred Roos stepped in. If Lucas hadn't let go of his initial idea of making Han Solo into a sort of green monster, maybe Harrison Ford would have remained the carpenter to the stars. But, the director wanted a "human" for the role of the irresistible, funny, smug mercenary. Fred Roos knew that Lucas was looking for a new face and didn't want to hire an actor from *American Graffiti*. Nevertheless, the casting director was willing to stake everything on his favorite. What if, by pure chance, Ford the carpenter came to repair a door at the production offices, and it just happened to be where George Lucas was holding the auditions?

Hundreds of actors competed for the three main roles. Lucas was meticulous and had very definite ideas about what he was looking for. He was assisted by a young director who was practically unknown at the time, Brian de Palma. At the time, he was casting Princess Leia. Naturally, he ran into the carpenter in the corridor, with whom he had maintained an excellent relationship since *American Graffiti*. Lucas asked him if he would feed lines to the actresses. Ford accepted, although he was disappointed not to be participating in the production. As always, he took his work seriously. So seriously that Lucas was finally won over. It was obvious that Han Solo was Ford, or that Ford was Han Solo—either way, Ford was hired. He would play the sexy, insolent, cynical, unforgettable hero. Finally, he was on his way. Carrie Fisher, the daughter of Eddy Fisher and Debbie Reynolds, would portray the princess and Mark Hamill would play the young Luke Skywalker. Finally, Sir Alec Guiness, the Shakespearean actor, would play the part of Obi-Wan Kenobi, the wise patriarch.

"As an actor, you spend all your time watching until suddenly, you're the one being watched."

T he adventure of *Star Wars* began in March 1976. George Lucas came up with dozens of versions of the script before starting filming. To help the three actors adapt, the director gave them permission to let their imaginations run wild. They took him up on it, sometimes altering their own dialog. Harrison was overflowing energy. "As Han Solo, Harrison was a free electron, out of orbit!" said Lucas. Most of the shooting was done in England at the Elstree Studios, but some was also done in the United States, North Africa, the Middle East, and Guatemala. The whole thing was shot in a little over two months–two months of suffering for Lucas.

Immediately after they arrived in Tunisia, it started to rain and refused to let up. It hadn't rained like that in fifty years! Then, of course, a sandstorm hit. When the exteriors were finally finished, the crew returned to England where everyone was looking forward to cool weather, but what they got was the heat wave of the century! Although Lucas had a wonderful relationship with his three main stars, Alec Guinness was another story. Guiness thought his role was too small. He didn't appear until halfway through the film and then died, albeit heroically, shortly thereafter. Lucas argued with him and tried to play it down. What Guinness didn't know was that Lucas actually preferred his robots. They were his main characters. C-3PO and R2-D2 were his favorites. What could you do? "Lucas would have loved to make the film with nothing but machines and no actors," says Mark Hamill. On May 25, 1977, the film was released in theaters in the U.S., and the *Star Wars* phenomenon was underway.

Han Solos and C-3PO (Star Wars, 1977)

In three months, it took in 100 million dollars. It was nominated for ten Oscars and won eight, for special effects, art direction, costumes, music, and sound effects, but none for the actors. That didn't stop all the boys from wanting to look like Luke Skywalker and all the girls from falling in love with Han Solo. Ford was not, as might be feared, the foil of Mark Hamill. The press even began comparing him to John Wayne. He didn't think any more about it. The love letters and autograph signings, all went over his head. He had fun but didn't get caught up in the game. "As an actor, you spend all your time watching until suddenly, you're the one being watched." Nevertheless, his dream had become a reality. As soon as the film was released, he went back to Mary and his two children, whom he'd hardly seen in recent months. Too bad for the paparazzis. It would be quite a while before Harrison Ford would make it to the tabloids.

With Mark Hamill (Luke Skywalker)

While he was still playing Han Solo in *Star Wars*, Francis Ford Coppola invited Harrison Ford to join him on the bustling stage of *Apocalypse Now*. The director wanted him for an important role. The actor was tempted, because he knew the film would be fabulous. But the very idea of spending months in the Philippines made him uneasy. Filming had begun one year earlier and everything had gone wrong. With illnesses, changes in casting, Martin Sheen's heart attack, and the demands of Marlon Brando, it was a nightmare. Harrison, who was aware of all this, agreed to participate on one condition: he would act in only one small scene. He would not agree to be stranded on the other side of the world! So Coppola offered him the part of a young officer named, coincidentally, Colonel G. Lucas. He appears at the very beginning of *Apocalypse Now*, so briefly that few people in the audience would recognize him. He was made even less recognizable by the fact that his head was shorn and he was wearing a pair of unflattering glasses. Ford was supposed to be gone for a week, but he managed to return after four days, happy to have avoided the worst. On the other hand, it was time well spent. While shooting, he had met a young assistant, the charming Melissa Mathison.

Force 10 From Navaronne (1978)
with Robert Shaw

There he was, practically unknown and almost rich (*Star Wars* earned him $55,000). Oddly enough, Harrison Ford didn't just take any role that was offered to him. He was more than satisfied with a good part that was well written. One project that grabbed his attention dealt with veterans returning from Vietnam and trying to rebuild their lives. The film was called Heroes and his co-star was Henry Winkler, the famous TV star who played Fonzie in *Happy Days*. The film was directed by Jeremy Paul Kagan, a close friend of George Lucas. Heroes brought Ford neither fame nor fortune, but he loved his character, a brave kid from Missouri with a head full of dreams. Although the critics praised his performance, the film itself didn't do well at the box office. This didn't discourage Harrison. He was becoming more and more attached to his acting career and less and less attached to carpentry. Next, he was offered a part in Force Ten from Navarone, directed by Guy Hamilton (to whom we owe several James Bond movies). Filming began in October 1977 in Yugoslavia. Ford was extremely bored. The critics panned the film, but it was no longer Harrison's problem.

And always behind the scenes was Mary. She accepted her husband's long absences because it was all for a good cause. Ford had finally penetrated Hollywood. Nevertheless, the couple was having trouble. Might this have been the main reason behind Harrison's departure for England to play a starring role in *Hanover Street*? He agreed to cross the Atlantic to portray an American bomber pilot, and it's understandable that he might want to flee a difficult family environment. For once, maybe he also wanted to play a romantic lead. "I'd yet to kiss a girl or be involved romantically." Now he would be able to put his arms around Lesley-Anne Down, a pretty British actress, and this was a pleasing prospect. So he left his wife and children for several months. The filming itself remains for him a painful memory. He didn't get along with the director, Peter Hyams, he thought the film wasn't very good and, no doubt, he was pessimistic about the future of his marriage. It was a bad period in his life. He would never want to hear this film mentioned again. Neither would the audience!

Frisco Kid (1979) with Gene Wilder

Harrison then followed it up with *The Frisco Kid*, with Gene Wilder. During filming, he negotiated with George Lucas for the second *Star Wars* movie. Unlike Mark Hamill and Carrie Fisher, he had never agreed to a sequel. Harrison insisted that Han Solo become a deeper, more "human" character. He would get his wish. Lucas would turn the intrepid mercenary into a sensitive and amorous hero. The actor was sold on the idea, all the more because he was offered a percentage of the profits. If this film did as well as the first, Harrison would never have to worry about money again! The trio was reunited. The movie would be called *The Empire Strikes Back*. *The Frisco Kid*, which was released in 1979, didn't exactly draw crowds. The actor was filled with self-doubt. What if he was an actor who could only do one role? Was Han Solo becoming too big?

Business discussion between Han Solo and Jabba the Hut

This time, it was divorce. Mary and Harrison finally separated in 1979. Their two sons (10 and 12) would live with their mother in the house Harrison had built, while he moved into an apartment. It was discovered that for two years, he had often been seen in the company of a young screenwriter. Fred Roos (the actor certainly owes him a lot!) was the one who brought them back together after the filming of *Apocalypse Now*. Melissa Mathison, intelligent and independent, did not appear to be a mere fling.

But, Ford would always credit Mary with supporting him ("She never once reproached me"), and with following him wherever he went so he would never have to spend too much time away from his children. For a long time, he blamed the movie business for the breakup of his first marriage.

Scandinavian storm

A new *Star Wars* episode was now underway, and off to a bad start. Mark Hamill was in a car accident and had to undergo several rounds of plastic surgery (which is why the film starts out with the young hero wounded and put in the bacta tank!). Lucas, worn out from filming the first episode, passed the baton to Irvin Kershner, who took over as director. In March 1979, the entire crew departed for Scandinavia. The script written by Lucas (and by Lawrence Kasdan) required that the first scenes be shot in a violent storm. They got their wish! Norway was immediately hit by a blizzard, much to the dismay of the actors and technicians who had some difficult moments. As always, Harrison was bursting with ideas. He sometimes suggested changes to the dialog. Kirshner was initially skeptical, but let him have his way. Thus, when Princess Leia told Han Solo that she loved him, he was supposed to reply "I love you, too." Ford suggested changing it to "I know," which was more in line with the shy and instant character of the egotistical mercenary. Bingo! This reply would become a favorite of Star Wars fans.

Romantic scene fans have been waiting for

The end of Han Solo? (The Empire Strikes Back, 1980

Lucas was uneasy. Could the sequel to a legendary film really succeed? And what if the audience was tired of intergalactic battles? The initial budget of 10 million dollars was exceeded. The *Empire Strikes Back* had to work. He left to spend a few days in Hawaii with his friend Steven Spielberg. Spielberg was telling him about his dream of directing a sort of cross between James Bond and Tarzan, a real adventure film. Lucas cut him off. "I have just what you need." For years, Lucas had been working on an idea, the story of a foolhardy archeologist along the lines of heroes from the 1930s. The two men were hooked. You never know when or where a project will take shape. It can even happen on a beach on the other side of the world.

The second *Star Wars* film was released in the U.S. on May 21, 1980. From the very first day, lines extended around the block. There were stories of people standing in line up to twelve hours just to be able to get into the theaters. It was a phenomenal success that brought in 233 million dollars in the U.S. alone. Once again, the Force was with them! Audiences remained faithful to Luke, Leia, and Han. But, one question continued to haunt the fans: the movie ended with Solo frozen. Would he die? The suspense would leave Harrison Ford plenty of time to reflect on his future. Maybe he would make a third episode, or maybe not. One thing was certain: he had to find a role that was opposite to the one he played in *Stars Wars*, a role where he would have both feet on the ground, far from the stars. In any case, Harrison knew that he would never play another epic hero. Who could possibly compete with Han Solo?

The famous Lucas-Spielberg project began to take shape. Lawrence Kasdan assisted in writing the script one more time, and the two friends, Lucas and Spielberg embarked on a "risky" venture, risky because it didn't follow any trend. Studios were refusing to produce this UFO. Tired of arguing, Paramount finally gave in. Spielberg and Lucas agreed that Spielberg would direct the film alone. He asked only one thing of his friend the producer: "Are you sure you want to call your archeologist Indiana Smith?" Lucas insisted on Indiana. It was the name of his wife's dog. As for Smith, he was open to suggestions. So Spielberg decided on Jones and took it from there. The choice of a main actor was crucial. He had to be a Bogart, an Errol Flynn, or possibly a Gary Cooper. Spielberg's first thought was Harrison Ford. He had never met him, but he sensed an adventurer's spirit in Han Solo. Lucas was opposed. The public would be confused and would never be able to distinguish between the two heroes, one in the stars and the one on the ground. Besides, Ford had already starred in two of his films. "I don't want to make him my Robert De Niro," he said, referring to Martin Scorcese who, at the time, was using De Niro in all his films. They considered Nick Nolte, then Peter Coyote. Screen tests were inconclusive. Then they had the brilliant idea of hiring Tom Selleck, the star of *Magnum, P.I.*, the hit TV series. He was perfect for the part, passed the audition and was hired immediately. Whew! Filming could begin. But, they didn't count on Selleck's iron-clad contract with CBS. Despite prolonged negotiations with the series' producers, the actor couldn't get out of it. They would have to fall back on someone else. Spielberg knew that Harrison Ford was what they needed. Lucas allowed himself be convinced.

Steven Spielberg didn't know Ford. They would have to meet and talk. The stakes were high. The two men appreciated one another and both would do good work. Harrison was adamant about one point—he must be guaranteed three films. As with *Star Wars,* he had his doubts. If he still needed a shove in the right direction, his companion Melissa would oblige. She knew this could be the chance Harrison was waiting for. So he would be Indiana Jones, and three times, if need be.

In June of 1980, the entire crew flew to England. Lucas, who was superstitious, wanted to start filming at Elstree Studios (where *Star Wars* was shot). Harrison trained hard. He had to learn how to wield a whip and to be in perfect physical shape. Not being especially athletic, he took great pains to be credible as a professor, a man of action, and a ladies' man. Paramount had warned Spielberg that if he went over his 20-million-dollar budget, they would pull the plug. The director was under pressure. Everything had to be calculated down to the last penny. Spielberg wasn't born yesterday, he knew unforeseen circumstances would arise. But he had no idea how right he was.

The crew then traveled to Tunisia which, for the sake of convenience, would serve as 1930s Egypt. Everyone stayed in a hotel and ate the excellent dishes provided—all except Spielberg, who had his own food shipped from the U.S. He would be the only one not to fall ill during filming. Without exception, all the actors and technicians contracted an extreme form of dysentery, unlike any the Tunisians had ever seen before. Harrison was no exception. He suffered through the most dangerous scenes. He never complained and Spielberg would be grateful to him.

One of the scenes in the script required that Indiana battle an evil Egyptian with a saber. They rehearsed the fight for over a week. When the day finally arrived, Ford wasn't feeling up to it. He went to see the director and said, "I couldn't fight this guy for hours to save my life." "Well, what do you want to do?" "I'll shoot him with my pistol." No sooner said than done. Indiana shot down the poor stuntman who had trained long and hard to be the perfect adversary. All he could do was put away his saber and go home. The crew died laughing. Spielberg, seeing the reaction, knew he had to keep the scene, and Harrison saved them four days of shooting. Later on, Indiana had to fight a Nazi right next to a plane. The actor lost his balance and his leg was trapped under a wheel. It took forty men to free him. He came away with only a severed ligament, but almost lost his leg. They did their best to care for him with the resources they had, which were somewhat limited, given that they were in the heart of Tunisia.

Contrary to what you may have heard, Indiana Jones was the one who was afraid of snakes, not Harrison Ford. Only one thing bothered him, as Spielberg soon learned. "When we started shooting a scene where Harrison had to dive into the water, he grimaced. Of course, he didn't say anything, but I knew I was putting him through hell!" Harrison Ford did not like getting wet, but he would jump twenty meters and remain nose-to-nose with a snake for two hours without budging. Sometimes he got hurt. The insurance company would no longer allow him to risk his life and no fewer than four stand-ins had to take turns. In the end, Harrison only had to brave one waterfall while holding onto his hat, an essential prop that flew off at the least provocation. Exasperated, he finally stapled it to his head, before the astonished eyes of the technicians.

Lucas visited the set in Tunisia. The director of *Star Wars* inserted a private joke for his fans: informed viewers will note that some of the hieroglyphics are effigies of R2-D2 and C-3PO. Melissa Mathison also came to visit her friend. There she met Spielberg, who knew her as the young woman who had just written the script for *The Black Stallion*. He told her about his new project, the story of a small extraterrestrial who gets lost on the way home to his planet. She was enthralled by the idea and offered to collaborate on the writing, a decision she would never regret.

"When we started shooting a scene where Harrison had to dive into the water, he grimaced. Of course, he didn't say anything, but I knew I was putting him through hell!"

During the filming, the small monkey Snuff, turned out to be the most capricious "actor" of them all.

Harrison slipped happily into the character of Indiana Jones. "More tortured, more intelligent than Han Solo, he's a taciturn guy with a wry sense of humor who's a lot like me." Spielberg liked that the actor knew how to "suffer, be afraid, cry. He gives the audience permission to be Indiana Jones, too." The film was released on June 12, 1981, one year after shooting started. Altogether, it earned 355 million dollars worldwide and won four Oscars, though still nothing for Ford, who wasn't even nominated. But now no one doubted him, especially the public, who awarded him many other prizes, including one for popularity. He became the only actor to portray two epic heroes. Directors in Hollywood had good reason to remember him.

A character directly inspired by sit-coms from the 50s

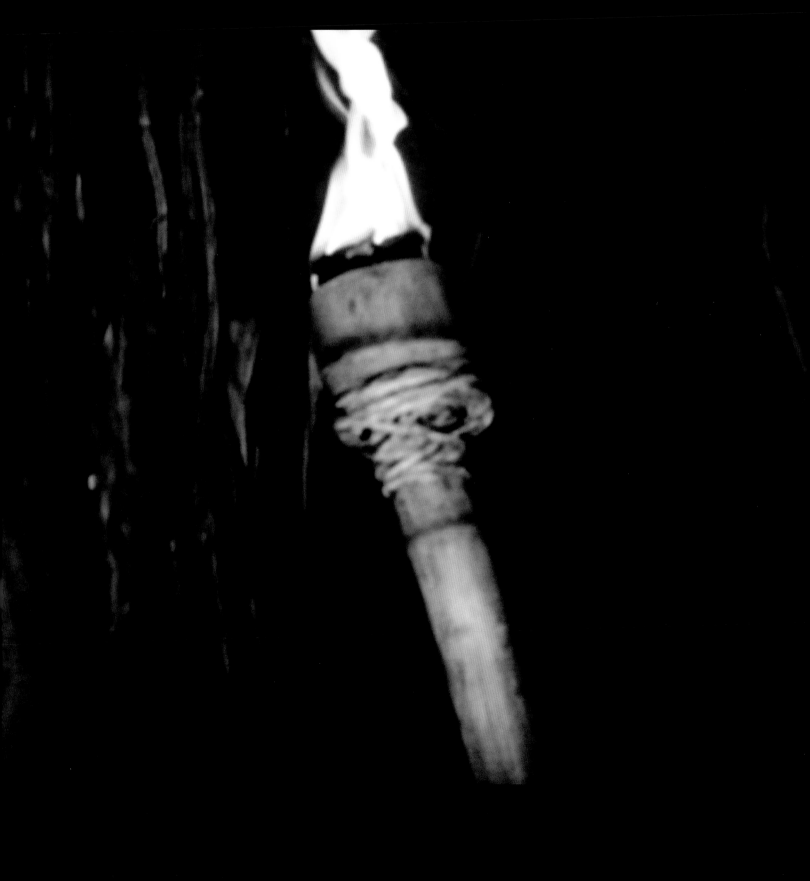

Ridley Scott, still coming off the success of *The Duellists*, knew that Harrison Ford would be ideal for *Blade Runner.* This futuristic and visually sophisticated film is the story of a Philip-Marlowe-style gumshoe who's hunting for "replicants." He's dark and hard and, for Harrison, his best opportunity to show a different side of his talent. He decided to alter himself physically. He didn't want people to see Han Solo or Indiana Jones. He put on an oversized jacket and cut his hair short, making himself look like Elvis Costello, his older son Benjamin's favorite rock star. He also agreed to do the film for personal reasons. It would be shot near his children's school. Even though he was on good terms with his first wife, he missed his kids.

It's no secret that relations between the director and actor were strained. They couldn't agree on the script. Ridley Scott saw Rick Deckard (played by Ford) as a robot disguised as a man. Harrison, on the other hand, wanted to "be human" so the audience could identify with him. For the first time, Harrison was unhappy shooting. "This was the most difficult film I've ever done," he would say years later. And, although Ford has thick skin, he was bothered by the fact that Scott was so much more interested in his sets than in his actors. *Blade Runner* wasn't really a flop, but it wasn't a hit either. With time, it would become a cult film, and in a survey of the sixty greatest scientists in the world, it would be named the best science fiction film ever made.

Harrison, on the other hand, wanted to "be human"
so the audience could identify with him.

While bravely promoting *Blade Runner*, Harrison was preparing to be thawed. He would once again play Han Solo. He had agreed to shoot the last chapter of *Star Wars*, called *Return of the Jedi*. Lucas chose Richard Marquand, a Welsh filmmaker and former actor, to direct. Proper precautions were taken during shooting. Fearing the intrusion of fans on the plateau in Arizona, the producers came up with a stratagem. Harrison would be supposed to be shooting a low-budget horror film called *Blue Harvest*. As for the film crew of *Star Wars 3*, they would fly to Germany. However, they underestimated the press. Two weeks into the shooting, the *Los Angeles Times* uncovered the plot and fans poured in from all four corners of the United States to catch a glimpse of their idols. These were the same fans who whooped with joy (an understatement) when the film was released and Han Solo took up his role in the first scenes. *Return of the Jedi* was sure to be a spectacular success, and all the more spectacular because the audience knew it would be the final chapter in the trio's adventures. That was the end. Harrison Ford said a final farewell to Han Solo.

Return of the Jedi, (1983).
With Mark Hamill

Harrison Ford was never without work. He had barely finished filming *Return of the Jedi* when he began his second Indiana Jones adventure. Melissa Mathison hadn't lost any time, either. Steven Spielberg's *E.T.* had just been filmed (Ford played a small role that was cut during editing) and she had written the script. At 32, she became an important figure in Hollywood, and she owed none of it to the man in her life. This is undoubtedly one of the reasons they got along so well. Harrison and Melissa were said to be the "ideal couple." Hollywood loves perfect romances and it would not be disappointed.

On March 14, 1983, news agencies around the world would broadcast the announcement of their wedding in Santa Monica. They had just enough time to move to Wyoming. Their honeymoon would have to wait. Ford had to run off to Sri Lanka to begin shooting *Indiana*

Screenwriter Melissa Mathison and husband, actor Harrison Ford

Jones and the Temple of Doom. Harrison was afraid that filming would be anything but restful. Indeed, a month after he took up his hat and whip for the second time, he was hospitalized in Los Angeles. He couldn't endure sitting on the back of an elephant for hours at a time. The diagnosis was undeniable: two herniated disks and six weeks of mandatory rest—rest that cost the production one million dollars. Afterwards, Harrison returned as though nothing had happened. "As soon as I knew that if I fell, I had a pretty good chance of being able to get up again, I didn't worry about it."

The reviews were mixed. The element of surprise was gone. On top of all that, the MPAA in the U.S. had rated it PG-13, apparently because of gratuitous violence. Despite this difficult blow, the *Temple of Doom* was a hit. There's no age limit when it comes to loving Indiana Jones.

*Ambiguous face off between Harrison
and Kelly McGillis in* Witness *(1985)*

Peter Weir was desperate. Just as he started preproduction of *The Mosquito Coast,* which was based on a novel by Paul Theroux, the backers abandoned the project. Disgusted, the Australian director returned home. Two weeks later, he was asked to direct *Called Home,* an unusual film because it takes place in a very religious, Amish community still living as though in the eighteenth century. Weir was enthusiastic, except for the fact that he was expected to work with Harrison Ford. It was the star who had sought out the director of *The Year of Living Dangerously* and wanted to work with him. The two men first had to meet and, of course, found that they got along. Ford invited Peter Weir to his ranch in Jackson Hole, Wyoming. The director felt a little awkward because he'd never seen any of Ford's films. Together, they spent days and nights discussing the role of the cop disoriented by his new life with the Amish. But, that wasn't all. "Harrison Ford doesn't think about anything but his character. He also had very relevant ideas about the script. If I was the pilot, he was a sort of copilot," says Weir.

To prepare for his role in Witness, which was the final title of the film, Harrison spent two weeks with the chief of Philadelphia homicide. The actual shooting began in April of 1984. In honor of his carpenter past, one of the most beautiful scenes in the movie involves the cop John Book and his new companions building a barn. There was no need for a stand-in. Harrison knew how to roof. He also said he wasn't feeling very disoriented. "Today, I live two different ways: like the Amish when I'm at home in Wyoming and like the policeman I portray when I'm in an urban environment." Perhaps that's why it's still considered to be Harrison Ford's best role. His friend Spielberg would say that he had "never seen him as vulnerable as he was in that film." The film was a triumph, and more popular with women than with men. In May 1985, Witness went to Cannes, where it was shown out of competition. Attendees watched as a reduced, ill-at-ease Indiana Jones pulled up in front of the Festival Palace, so distracted that he almost fell down the

John Book, as cop amongst the Amish, with Alexander Godunov, the young Lukas Haas and Jan Rubes

famous stairs! Truly, such worldly festivities were not for him, but he had to show up because, for the first time, Harrison Ford was nominated for an Oscar for *Witness*. In the end, William Hurt won the statuette for *Kiss of the Spider Woman*, but it made no difference. Recognition by his peers was not his problem. At 43, he much preferred to continue being the man in the street. He still considered it a miracle that he was able to act and be successful.

"Harrison Ford doesn't think about anything but his character. He also had very relevant ideas about the script. If I was the pilot, he was a sort of copilot," says Weir.

Ford and McGillis are nominated for Golden Globes awards, for their roles in Witness.

Mosquito Coast *(1986) Harrison Ford's favorite film*

It also felt miraculous to be able to turn down a project, or to initiate one on his own. Harrison Ford saw his chance. He was the one who sought out Peter Weir. Did the director still dream of making *The Mosquito Coast*? Then he would make it, though not with Jack Nicholson, as he originally planned, but with Harrison. For the first time, the actor would play an unsympathetic character. He was warned that portraying the father of a family who's lost his mind could endanger his career. Regardless, he would be Allie Fox, a crazy man in his forties with a wild eye, worlds away from the characters Harrison had played up until then. This man who abandoned his comfortable American life to embark on an adventurous existence had a number of things in common with the actor. Admittedly, Wyoming was no Mosquito Coast, but we can understand

the attraction for the actor, who was more and more put off by Hollywood. The British actress

Helen Mirren played his wife. She was a little intimidated by Harrison, which was all the better,

since Peter Weir needed her to feel anxious and even frightened by her husband. The son would

be played by the young River Phoenix, whom Ford took under his wing.

The Mosquito Coast: Hilary Gordon, River Phoenix, Harrison Ford, and Helen Mirren, 1986.

With John Sloane, Camera Man

Shooting began in Belize, Central America, where the heat was devastating. The film lived up to its name. The crew was literally assaulted by gangs of mosquitoes. The public was expecting a miracle from Peter Weir, but it didn't materialize. Harrison Ford's favorite film (as he says in every interview) was a flop. Not only did the critics pan it, but the public didn't bother to see it. This was a devastating blow for an actor who had put so much of himself into the film. Obviously, there were no Oscar nominations, neither for him nor for the director. For the first time in his career, Ford complained to the press: "I have never seen a serious film treated so badly by the critics. And I think they're wrong." He returned to Wyoming feeling extremely angry. Melissa was able to console him, however, with news of the approaching birth of their first child.

A pregnant Melissa left for Paris, where she was supposed to meet with the Polish director, Roman Polanski. Together they wanted to create an adaptation of *Tintin*, the comic strip by Hergé. Harrison, upset by the idea of his wife traveling a Paris, that had recently been traumatized by a spate of terrorist bombings, decided to accompany her. So he naturally made the acquaintance of the controversial director, who was banned from traveling in the U.S. after being implicated in a scandal. Although the *Tintin* project never came to fruition, Polanski was fascinated by the scriptwriter's husband. At dinner, the director described for the actor a script he had in mind. "Described," puts it a little mildly. Although Harrison didn't understand a word of French and Polanski's English was limited, his talent for gesturing was extraordinary. Standing on a table, the director gesticulated vigorously, portraying all the characters in his "Hitchcockian" thriller with verve. Harrison was spellbound and immediately accepted Polanski's proposal.

In *Frantic,* he would play an American surgeon searching for his kidnapped wife in Paris. Filming began in May of 1987. Baby Malcolm, born two months earlier, accompanied his parents to France. Polanski was immediately taken aback by the actor, who discussed, argued, and offered ideas. This was not at all what the director of *Rosemary's Baby* had in mind. For the star, being lost in a city where he understood neither the language nor the mentality, it wasn't a difficult role to embody. He was astonished by the way filming was done, worlds away from anything he had ever experienced before. "In France, you wake up at 11:00 a.m. and arrive on the set at 1:00 p.m. after a lunch of wining and dining, completely plastered. You film until 9:00 p.m., dine until 11:00 p.m., and then go to a nightclub. Since I was playing a man who was always exhausted, it helped me a lot." Harrison's discipline initially took a blow, but he soon got into the swing of things and, despite appearances, the two men got on well. For Polanski, Harrison Ford, was Gary Cooper, "straightforward, outspoken and vulnerable."

Frantic *(1988), with director Roman Polanski, always quite dramatic.*

In Paris, Harrison met Clint Eastwood, who was in the process of filming *Bird*. They returned to the United States together. It was a strange trip for several reasons. The plane, after suffering from serious technical difficulties, made an emergency landing in Maine. A little sooner and Hollywood would have permanently lost two of its most popular actors. *Frantic* was released in the U.S. in February 1988 and Harrison Ford scored another victory. The press was unanimous in saluting his performance.

Fifteen years later in 2003, Harrison Ford accepted the Oscar for best director that Roman Polanski won for *The Pianist*. It just goes to show that even in the movie business, friendships can last.

Working Girl by Mike Nichols with Harrison Ford, Melanie Griffith and Sigourney Weaver, 1988

And how about if he tried his hand at comedy? Mike Nichols, director of *The Graduate* who had passed over Harrison in favor of Dustin Hoffman, asked him to play a minor character in *Working Girl*. His co-star would be Melanie Griffith. After the exhausting work of filming *Frantic*, he was looking for something a little lighter. He accepted the part on the condition that his role be made more substantial. He was a last-minute replacement for Alec Baldwin, who was initially considered for the role. The actor felt right at home in this story about manipulation on Wall Street. He even had the impression that he was "playing the role of the woman. Melanie Griffith is the man of the film. All I have to do is let myself be carried along." For the first time in his career, the famous scar on Harrison's chin became part of the story. In one scene, Nichols had Melanie Griffith ask him where it came from. He first convinced her that he got it in violent, macho fight, but then he thought the better of it and admitted that he injured himself on a toilet seat. Harrison had a good time. Nichols would call him "the Ferrari of actors." "Probably because I'm expensive and high-maintenance." Only Sigourney Weaver had a problem during filming. She complained that Ford was being paid twice as much as her for a role of equal duration. Harrison was nominated for a Golden Globe in the best actor category and, as an added bonus, the film was a huge success when it was released in the U.S. in December of 1988.

Working Girl was a vacation. No fighting, no climbing, meaning that Harrison was rested enough to return to his role as Indiana Jones for Spielberg.

It was now 1989 and Jeffrey Boam's script was almost finished. The legendary hero was returning to his past, when he was 14 years old. The adolescent Indiana was portrayed by River Phoenix, who Harrison had met on the set of *The Mosquito Coast*. Spielberg found a new explanation for the now "legendary" scar. We learn that Indiana—"Indy" to his friends—injured himself with his own whip! Twenty-six years later, the hero's father, the honorable Henry Jones, disappears and the son immediately goes in search of him. But who would play the gruff, somewhat eccentric, occasionally authoritarian father, a man capable of having sired such a foolhardy progeny? Spielberg was a dreamer. He wanted to find an actor worthy of Indiana. "Other than James Bond, I can't see anyone doing it," he said. So it would have to be James Bond himself–Sean Connery. Connery was only twelve years older than Harrison, but so what? Would Mr. Connery balk at such an insignificant detail? "I'm a lot younger than I look. I should play the role of Indy's sister." "You know Sean," cracked Harrison, "he can do anything, even father a child at age twelve." In the end, Indiana Jones and the *Last Crusade* was more about the father-son relationship than about any quest for the Grail. The audience was in heaven. Spielberg, like everyone else, was already dreaming up a fourth episode.

"I finally see
life from a
different angle.
In the clouds,
I'm a
responsible
being."

When he was very young, Harrison Ford already dreamed of piloting an airplane. He took a few flying lessons, but soon quit due to a lack of money. Now almost 50 and earning around 12 million dollars per film, Harrison was making a decent living, to say the least. It was enough to become a seasoned pilot and he wasted no time. In 1996, he got his pilot's license and bought himself a mini-fleet of six planes and one helicopter, which allowed him to fly from his ranch in Wyoming to Hollywood or New York whenever he wanted. "I finally see life from a different angle. In the clouds, I'm a responsible being." In the air, he was on his own and, even better, he could save lives. Indeed, in August 2000, the Wyoming police received an alarming message that a 20-year-old woman was reported missing at an altitude of 3000 meters. Without hesitation, Harrison landed his helicopter and rescued the dehydrated woman. "Do you recognize me?" her rescuer asked. "Not at all," she responded. It's one of the hazards of being number one at the box office. A year later, he rescued a 13-year-old boy scout lost in the woods. And to think that some critics claim Harrison Ford is too old to play Indiana Jones for a fourth time.

Harrison Ford flies his helicopter,
July 10, 2001 Near Jackson, Wy.
Ford located and rescued missing
13-Year-old Boy Scout Cody Clawson.

After Alec Baldwin, Harrison becomes the famous Jack Ryan in War Games,*(1992), by Tom Clancy.*

The 1980s were a turning point in Harrison Ford's career. He was almost 50 and good roles were not just falling into his lap. Nor was the actor making the best choices, starring in a series of films that would never make cinematic history. *Presumed Innocent* was a decent thriller. *Regarding Henry* was an Oscar-winning role (though he didn't win one). In this film, he was reunited with Mike Nichols to play a cynical lawyer who sustains a brain injury during a holdup and loses his memory, but regains his soul. The film was released in September 1991. At the same time, Ford came in eleventh in the list of the richest actors in Hollywood, which meant he was now probably earning more than $150 dollars a week.

Hollywood had discovered Tom Clancy. This master of the spy novel had already had his work adapted for the screen in 1990 with *The Hunt for Red October.* Alec Baldwin portrayed the notorious Jack Ryan, a James-Bond type, but without his sense of humor. At the time, Harrison Ford had turned down the project. He would have accepted a secondary role as the Russian captain, but wasn't given the chance—it went instead to his movie "father," Sean Connery.

Since Paramount had bought the rights to three adaptations, there were two more to go. So one year later, preproduction began on *Patriot Games.* This time Ford was interested. Exit Alec Baldwin who, understandably, didn't take it very well. This was the second time he'd lost a role to Harrison, even though Ford was extremely expensive. But it was what the producers wanted, to the great displeasure of Clancy, who considered him to be too old. But, Ford would play Jack Ryan, and twice, since he also played him in *Clear and Present Danger* in 1994. In the end, audiences preferred Ford's interpretation to Baldwin's, and Tom Clancy had to give in.

In 1990, Melissa Mathison gave birth to Georgia, Harrison Ford's first daughter. Like her brother Malcolm, she would be raised at the Jackson Hole ranch and brought up to love nature. Although Harrison was the ultimate nonconformist, he became one of the greatest defenders of the environment, along the lines of a Robert Redford. He is an active member of Conservation International. Thanks to his efforts, many animals that were headed for extinction have been saved. Harrison Ford will never be totally consumed by the cause, but conservationists still insisted on honoring him by asking him to name a species of butterfly, which he chose to call Georgia. Later on, the American Museum of Natural History named a California spider, *Calponia harrisonfordi.*

Harrison Ford speaks as the recipient of Harvard Medical School's 2002 Environmental Citizen Award May 13, 2002 at the New England Aquarium in Boston. Ford has served on the board of Conservation International for 10 years where he played a key role in the designing and development of CI's Center for Environmental Leadership in Business.

Harrison Ford during the 11th Annual
Benefit for the African Rainforest
Conservancy (ARC) at Jimmy's Uptown
in New York City. Mr. Ford named a
newly discovered species of Tanzanian
butterfly Georgia, after his daughter.

*Harrison Ford is Dr. Kimble
in* The Fugitive *(1993)*

When asked how he felt about *The Fugitive* TV series, which aired from 1963 to 1967, Harrison Ford replied that, "At that time, I preferred chasing girls to watching television." So it was totally without preconceptions that the actor embarked on this new project, the suspenseful story of Dr. Richard Kimble (originally played by David Jansen), unjustly accused of murdering his wife. Imprisoned and condemned to die in the electric chair, he manages to escape and goes in search of the real murderer. Director Andrew Davis knew that if this film was to succeed, it would only be due to the omnipresent Harrison. The actor spent many months poring over the script and offered to play the role of the cop who pursued him. The producers made the wise choice of giving the role of the brutal, but human policeman to Tommy Lee Jones. This duo would be crucial to the success of *The Fugitive*.

Nevertheless, it was no simple task. Following his escape, Dr. Kimble had to transform himself physically. But how to do it? The producers knew audiences were paying to see the real face of Harrison Ford, so they decided he would start the film with a beard. And that was it. Once he escaped, he would shave it off and his appearance would be changed. "I had a hard time seeing myself do a Peter Sellers act, with fake nose and glasses." The most spectacular scene was when the train derailed. Contrary to what one might think, they used a real train (on a private railway line) and not a model.

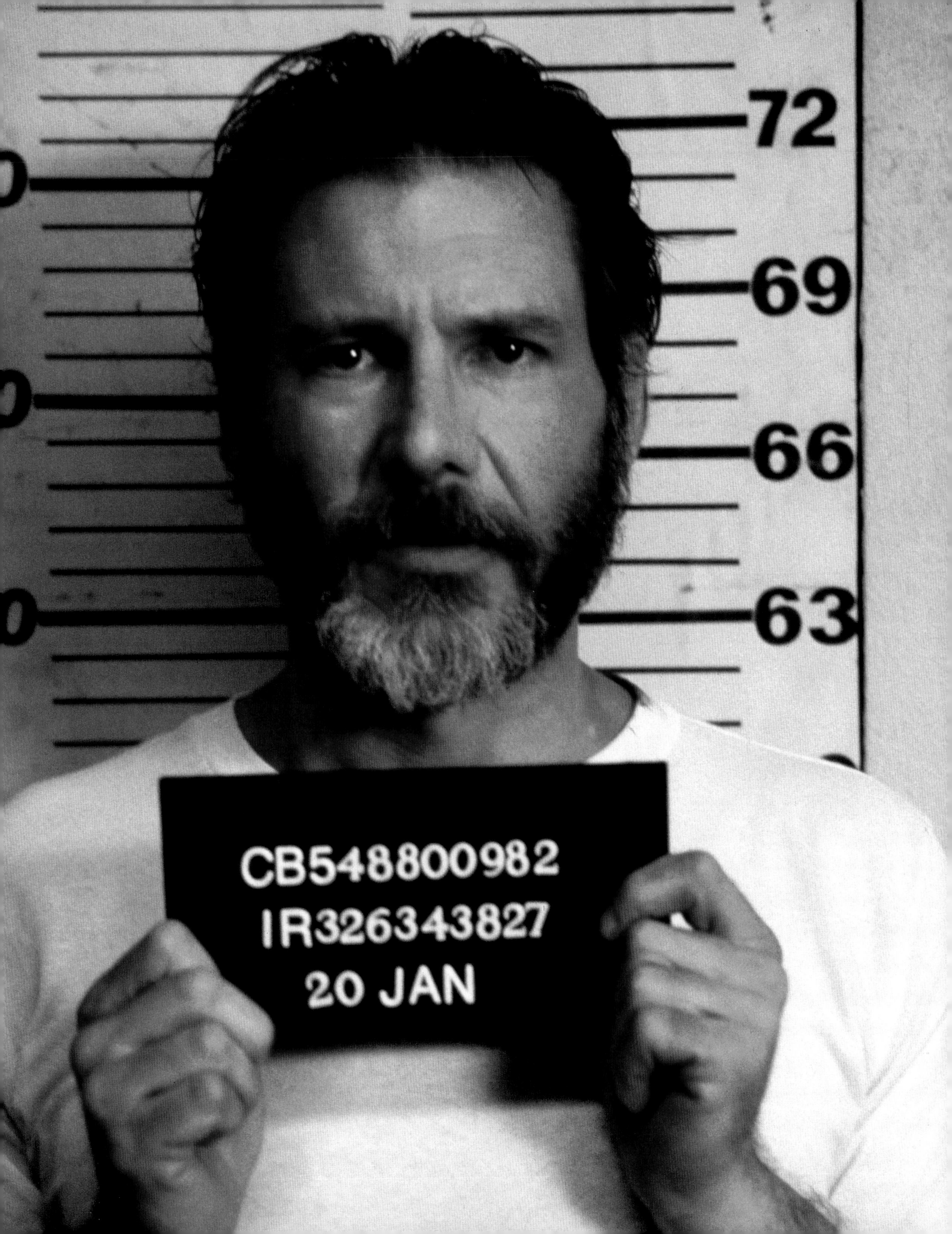
72
69
66
63
CB548800982
IR326343827
20 JAN

The Fugitive, *Harrison Ford's biggest success after* Star Wars *and* Indiana Jones

Audiences were bowled over by it, and many more by *The Fugitive* itself, one of the biggest blockbusters of 1993. The critics were once again in love with Harrison Ford. He was praised to the skies, which hadn't happened for quite some time. It was a great public and critical triumph. Harrison could return to Wyoming content. Later on, Harvard University accorded him the prize of Theatrical Man of the Year. It was Harvard's Hasty Pudding award, more of a student prank than a true honorary medal. Thus, he returned to the university stage, dressed in a bra and blond wig by the students. He accepted the award with his usual dignity, however, to roars of laughter from spectators who came in droves, and understandably so!

Harrison plays Humphrey Bogart's part in Sabrina *(1995). With Greg Kinnear and Julia Ormond.*

When cinema celebrated its hundredth anniversary, Harrison Ford was named Star of the Century for acting in the highest-grossing movies of all time. When complimented for it, however, he grimaced. "Do you really think that title means anything?" It was best to change the subject; for example, to *Sabrina*, the new Sidney Pollack film. People of all ages still remembered the adorable Audrey Hepburn in this 1954 Billy Wilder film. The remake was Ford's idea, and a cocky one. Maybe Harrison could make it as Humphrey Bogart, but Julia Ormond as Audrey Hepburn? Impossible. The remake was a dog, and the press had a field day. Nevertheless, Harrison was nominated for a Golden Globe, which was the only thing his fans would remember about *Sabrina*, despite their great affection for him.

Sometimes when you're a star, you get to meet the "real" president of the United States. Harrison Ford, in any case, dined with Bill Clinton in Jackson Hole, Wyoming, close to his ranch. "Could I have a look at Air Force One?" he asked Clinton, who was happy to oblige. It wasn't just that Harrison was an airplane buff who wanted to have a look at the machinery, but he was also preparing for a role as the president, taken hostage with his family on the famous Air Force One. Washington participated to some extent by offering the services of the Air Force. This opened the door for director Wolfgang Petersen to take a film crew onto air bases where they had previously been banned. Once again, Harrison would prove his talent as a stuntman. He was the first U.S. president to know how to throw real punches. Poor Gary Oldman, the bad guy in the movie, would never forget his fights with the Indiana Jones of the White House!

Air Force One brought in 166 million dollars, and Harrison joined the very exclusive circle of stars being paid $20 million per film. He celebrated the occasion by buying himself a gold ring. Damn! The classiest actor in Hollywood, faithful husband, doting father, and arch-enemy of glitz, wore a gold earring. Fans were beside themselves. It was the only thing the feverish press could talk about. "I didn't think anyone would notice, but it seems like it's the biggest thing I've ever done!" he joked. Nonetheless, People Magazine awarded him the title of sexiest actor on the planet, an honor he didn't take very seriously. It just goes to show how a little piece of jewelry can do wonders for your image.

Harrison, the "false" U.S. president on Air Force One (1997) meets the "real" Bill Clinton. With Tony Blair.

Gary Oldman, the terrorist

While filming The Devil's Own *(1997)
with Brad Pitt*

On a more serious note, Harrison Ford was wrapped up in a new project involving a militant Irish refugee in the United States. Brad Pitt had sent him a synopsis. Together, they chose Alan J. Pakula to direct. Right from the start, *The Devil's Own* was a tangle of problems. Pitt and Ford couldn't agree on the final script. When it came time to start shooting, only a quarter of the story had been written. Brad Pitt was in a panic. He'd never experienced these kinds of problems. He even threatened to quit, until the production company informed him that he would then have to pay sixty-million dollars in damages and interest. So the young actor settled down to work. Needless to say, the atmosphere on the set was strained. There was a lot of talk about bad blood between the two stars. Harrison has always denied the stories of constant fighting. He never put much stock in gossip. Pakula put an end to the rumors by talking about the great respect the two actors had for one another. It was appropriate to do so, since the subject of the film is the love between two men, an impossible love between father and son, as well as treason. Despite all the stories in the tabloids about pseudo-disagreements between the actors, *The Devil's Own* bombed in the U.S. A year later in 1998, Brad Pitt and Harrison Ford were reunited at a memorial service for Pakula, who was killed in an automobile accident. They refused to comment on the controversy.

When Martin Scorcese released *Kundun* in 1997, the Ford-Mathison couple was in the news. Melissa had written the script for this film, which dealt with the life of the Dalai Lama. Together, the couple took a stand on the side of Tibet and, along with Richard Gere, joined the ranks of Hollywood celebrities banned from entering China.

Harrison Ford (L) and wife Melissa Mathison Ford (R) pose with His Holiness Tenzin Gyatso, the Fourteenth Dalai Lama of Tibet, during a star-studded dinner in his honor 01 August in Beverly Hills, California. The event, during the Dalai Lama's week-long visit to the United States, raised money to help preserve the traditions of the Tibetan people.

Harrison Ford followed this up with *Six Days, Seven Nights*, a romantic comedy by Ivan Reitman and co-starring the charming Anne Heche. It's the story of a fashion editor stranded on a desert island after a plane crash. She's forced to share the island with a gruff pilot and, of course, falls in love with him. At 29, some critics found her a little young for Harrison. A number of young women, however, were well able to imagine themselves in the arms of the fifty-something actor. The two stars got along well and the shoot was idyllic. When the film was released, Anne Heche officially came out of the closet and announced her relationship with actress Ellen DeGeneres. America may have been shocked, but not Harrison, who supported his co-star to the end.

It's best to forget Ford's second and final collaboration with Sydney Pollack. Harrison swore that he would never again make a film with the director of *Out of Africa*. *Random Hearts*, which was released in October 1999, was a flop that couldn't be saved by the combined talents of Harrison and Kristin Scott Thomas, but the actor's future wasn't entirely gloomy. This time he was awarded the People's Choice Award as America's favorite actor. Once again, the public honored him. At 57, he was the sexiest and most popular actor in Hollywood.

What Lies Beneath (2000): First demonic personality for Harrison; with Michelle Pfeiffer

Harrison returned to the studios to play the shady husband of Michelle Pfeiffer in *What Lies Beneath* by Robert Zemeckis. It was a frightening thriller, a Hitchcock without Hitchcock. On February 17, 2000, the American Film Institute (AFI) decided to honor Harrison Ford with its famous Lifetime Achievement Award, adding him to the Institute's list of celebrated actors and directors that include: Clint Eastwood, Dustin Hoffman, Elizabeth Taylor, and Fred Astaire.

And then the unimaginable occurred. The indefatigable Ford took a break. Hollywood would have to get along without him, for a while anyway.

There was trouble at home. The relationship between Melissa Mathison and Harrison Ford was over. On November 7, 2000, the actor told the press that the legendary couple would be splitting up. Hollywood was in an uproar. You couldn't trust anyone anymore, not even the star, whom the tabloids were now accusing him of having an extramarital affair with actress Lara Flynn-Boyle. In a dramatic turn of events, the couple got back together two months later. The reconciliation didn't last long, however, and the divorce cost Harrison a fortune. Four years later, it was official. Melissa would have 85 million dollars as well as a percentage of all the films Ford made while they were married. It took a long time, but Harrison Ford was always a little slow. It took him 35 years to become famous and 58 to destroy the image. Fortunately Calista Flockhart, the beautiful Ally McBeal, was waiting in the wings. In 2002, she became Harrison's new companion. The actor was once again a settled man and Hollywood could breathe a sigh of relief.

In K19: The Widowmaker (2002).
Harrison becomes producer.

It was time to go back to work. After two years off, and a few troubles later, Harrison Ford was going to work with a woman director for the first time. Kathryn Bigelow persuaded the star to play the captain of the first Soviet nuclear submarine, whose reactor malfunctioned in the middle of the Cold War. It was a true story and so fascinated Ford that he became the producer of *K-19: The Widowmaker*. He would have complete power to impose his views. He would decide, for example, to assume a Russian accent despite his collaborators' reservations. He visited Russia with the director and met with the real sailors from the K-19.

These same sailors would later stir up a controversy. They felt the movie was insulting to them. They were heroes but, they complained, the film portrayed them as pirates and amateurs. The critics still liked it, but the movie was not as successful as anticipated. More attention was being paid to Ford's relationship with Calista Flockhart. She was by his side throughout the promotion of the film. Was Harrison's private life a target? "It's crazy. There's an obsession with celebrity. The tabloids stir up curiosity and then try to satisfy it." There would be no more quiet walks in New York or anywhere else. Like any other star, Harrison Ford was subject to harassment.

Nevertheless, he emerged from his lair once again. In 2002, Harrison came out of retirement to make *Hollywood Homicide* with Josh Hartnett, the hero of *Pearl Harbor.* It's a detective story that unfolds in the entertainment world. At nearly 60, Harrison was no longer playing young men. His character was short of breath, drank too much, and took Viagra. He had a good time with his image as an aging Romeo, "a sort of anti-Jack Ryan," he joked. But it was another bomb. Harrison Ford wasn't supposed to make fun of himself. His fans had no sense of humor. They wanted a superhero, perhaps even with a hat and whip. What a coincidence! Indiana Jones was on his way back.

Hollywood Homicide *(2003).*
Harrison acts his age. With
Josh Hartnett and Lena Olin

It's 2226th on the Hollywood Walk of Fame, right next to Spielberg's. The two men are inseparable. Everybody came to celebrate Harrison's star, including Calista and Harrison's mother. It was May 30, 2003, and he was about to turn 60. He didn't seem to be bothered by any of it. He was relaxed, smiling, and allowed his photo to be taken. It was all the same to Harrison. He was done getting angry, he was living the life he'd always wanted, both exciting and ordinary. Harrison Ford is a spoiled kid. He earns 25 million dollars per film and his fiancée is twenty years his junior. He's made over forty feature films and portrayed two legendary heroes. He has four children and two grandchildren. He's also been divorced twice, but nobody's perfect. He completed the movie *Firewall* in 2006. And, in 2007, he will make *Indiana Jones 4*. Spielberg had announced it. The crowd was ecstatic. Harrison smiled, or almost. Maybe he was nervous, maybe not. If we only knew what he was thinking. Was he thinking about that other star, a little further up on Hollywood Boulevard, that of the first Harrison Ford? The heartthrob of silent films who was so attractive to women, the star of black-and-white cinema, who died fifty years ago? The older actor has long been forgotten. His namesake is not ready to be. Harrison knows that lots of visitors confuse the two, and happily photograph the other Ford's star thinking it's his. For some reason, he finds it amusing.

Harrison Ford poses during a ceremony unveiling his star on the Hollywood Walk of Fame, May 30, 2003 in Hollywood.

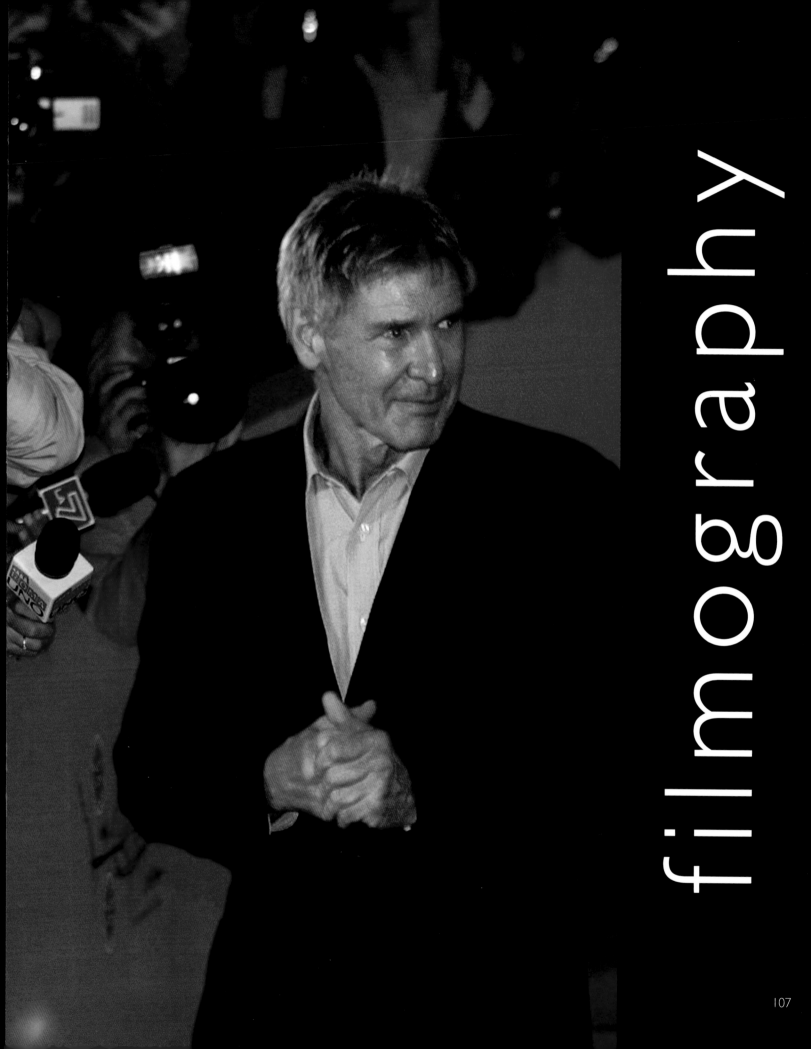

filmography

1966: Dead Heat On A Merry-Go-Round

(Bernard Girard)

1967: Luv

(Clive Donner)

1967: A Time for Killing

(Phil Karlson)

1968: Journey to Shiloh

(William Hale)

1970: Getting Straight

(Richard Rush)

1970: Zabriskie Point

(Michelangelo Antonioni)

1973 : American Graffiti

(George Lucas)

1974: The Conversation

(Francis Ford Coppola)

*US Actor Harrison Ford (C) beams
a large grin as Nick Gordon (L) and
Jason Watkins (R) plant a kiss on him
during the Hasty Pudding Theatrics
Man of the Year Award Presentation at
Harvard University, in Cambridge, MA,
20 February. Ford joins other notables
as Bob Hope, Clint Eastwood and Tom
Hanks as the Man of the Year.*

1977: Heroes

(Jeremy Paul Kagan)

1977: Star Wars

(George Lucas)

1978: Force Ten from Navarone

(Guy Hamilton)

1979: Apocalypse Now

(Francis Ford Coppola)

1979: The Frisco Kid

(Robert Aldrish)

1979: Hanover Street

(Peter Hyams)

1979: More American Graffiti

(Bill L. Norton)

1980: Empire Strikes Back

(Irvin Kershner)

Indiana Jones and the Temple of Doom

1981: Raiders of the Lost Ark

(Steven Spielberg)

1982: Blade Runner

(Ridley Scott)

1983: (Return of the Jedi

(Richard Marquand)

1984: Indiana Jones and the Temple of Doom

(Steven Spielberg)

1985: Witness

(Peter Weir)

1986: The Mosquito Coast

(Peter Weir)

1988: Frantic

(Roman Polanski)

1988: Working girl

(Mike Nichols)

With the people who discovered him:
Steven Spielberg and George Lucas

1989: Indiana Jones and the Last Crusade

(Steven Spielberg)

1990: Presumed Innocent

(Alan J. Pakula)

1991: Regarding Henry

(Mike Nichols)

1992: Patriot Games

(Philip Noyce)

1993: The Fugitive

(Andrew Davis)

1994: Clear and Present Danger

(Philip Noyce)

1995: Sabrina

(Sydney Polack)

1997: Air Force One

(Wolfgang Petersen)

Harrison Ford and Mark Hamill in Living Room

1997: The Devil's Own
(Alan J. Pakula)

1998: Six Days, Seven Night
(Ivan Reitman)

1999: Random Hearts
(Sydney Pollack)

2000: What Lies Beneath
(Robert Zemeckis)

2002: K-19, The Windowmaker
(Kathryn Bigelow)

2003: Hollywood Homicide
(Ron Shelton)

2006: Firewall
(Richard Loncraine)

2008: Indiana Jones 4
(Steven Spielberg)

May 1987, in Paris, while filming Frantic
by Roman Polanski

photographic credits

*After a 35 year career, Harrison Ford
remains one of Hollywood's biggest stars.*

Many thanks to:

Thémo Anargyros

Jean-Christophe Buisson

Alice Déon

Rodolphe Lachat